9   8   7   6   5   4   3
Digit on the right indicates the number of this printing.

ISBN 1–56138–755–X

Designed by Maria Taffera Lewis
Edited by Tara Ann McFadden
Printed in Hong Kong

This book may be ordered by mail from the publisher.
Please add $2.50 for postage and handling.
But try your bookstore first!

Running Press Book Publishers
125 South Twenty-second Street
Philadelphia, Pennsylvania 19103–4399

Simple Pleasures

A Journal of Life's Joys

RUNNING PRESS
PHILADELPHIA · LONDON

In character, in manners, in style, in all things,
the supreme excellence is simplicity.

Henry Wadsworth Longfellow

The man is the richest whose pleasures are the cheapest.

Henry David Thoreau

Simplicity is making the journey of this life with just baggage enough.

Charles Dudley Warner

*O*ne should start the day with a kiss.

Lawrence Sanders

He found himself whistling, stopped to wonder why,
and decided a nice day was a nice day.

John Sandford

Give me books, fruit, French wine, and fine weather and a little music out of doors, played by someone I do not know.

John Keats

It was all so condensed; everything was so simple
on the ice. It was just you, your stick and a couple of pucks.
The ice was crisp. My blades were sharp.
The air was cool and bracing, but I felt warm. That was life.

Eric Lindros

When I was six or seven years old, growing up in Pittsburgh, I used to take a precious penny of my own and hide it for someone else to find.

Annie Dillard

My advice is don't spend your money on therapy. Spend it in a record store.

Wim Wenders

It appears to me that it is the special province of music to move the heart.

Karl Phillip Emanuel Bach

Jazz will endure as long as people hear it through their feet instead of their brains.

John Phillip Sousa

I am always thirsting for beautiful, beautiful music.
I wish I could make it. Perhaps there isn't any music
on earth like what I picture to myself.

Olive Schreiner

The wonderful thing about music is that
it immediately evokes certain eras of one's life,
brings you back to where you've been. . . .

Donna de Matteo

There's a fantastic pleasure in being literally wrapped in sound, in having it go through your flesh and bones until your entire body is reverberating. You close your eyes and all your other senses are blacked out. There's only the perception of sound, but on a level above hearing. It's in your very being, but it has to be experienced to be understood.

Julius Faust

*d*ancing is the loftiest, the most moving, the most beautiful of the arts, because it is no mere translation or abstraction from life; it is life itself.

Havelock Ellis

He settled into a spot with room to stretch out his legs and he pulled his breakfast from the bag. A ride on a real train. The smell of good coffee. A comfortable seat. He smiled to himself as he unwrapped the bagel.

Darian North

The first fall of snow is not only an event,
it is a magical event. You go to bed
in one kind of world and wake up in another
quite different, and if this is not without
enchantment then where is it to be found?

John Boynton Priestly

The first weekend it goes below 40 degrees
I "celebrate" by baking bread from scratch. I love the tactile pleasure
of kneading the dough, the way my kitchen windows
get fogged up from the warmth of the oven and, of course,
the wonderful smell that fills the house.

Glamour **magazine**

I have bought bread and I have been given red roses:
how happy I am to hold both in my hand.

Kitahara Hakushu

A single conversation across the table with a wise man
is better than ten years' study of books.

Henry Wadsworth Longfellow

If you reveal your secrets thoughtlessly, they become burdens.
If you reveal them wisely, they become gifts.

Terry Hunt

Let tears flow of their own accord: their flowing
is not inconsistent with inward peace and harmony.
Lucius Annaeus Seneca

Half the pleasure of solitude comes
from having with us some friend to whom
we can say how sweet solitude is.

William Jay

It is very wonderful to see persons of the best sense passing hours together in shuffling and dividing a pack of cards with no conversation but what is made up of a few game-phrases, and no other ideas but those of black and red spots ranged together in different figures. Would not a man laugh to hear any one of his species complaining that life is short?

Joseph Addison

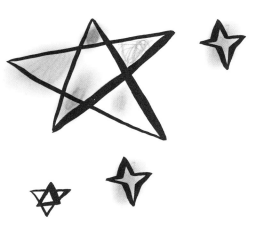

The joy of joys is the person of light but unmalicious humor.

Emily Post

. . . surrounding yourself with children
and their things is not a bad way at all to live
your life. They will make you happy,
they will make you laugh, and just when you think
you've seen or heard everything, they will
warm you heart with tenderness and love.

David Heller

always serve too much hot fudge sauce on hot fudge sundaes.
It makes people overjoyed, and puts them in your debt.

Judith Olney

Subtly, in the little ways, joy has been leaking
out of our lives. The small pleasures of the ordinary
day seem almost contemptible, and glance off us lightly. . . .
Perhaps it's a good time to reconsider pleasure at its roots.
Changing out of wet shoes and socks, for instance.
Bathrobes. Yawning and stretching. Real tomatoes.

Barbara Holland

She believes in basics—in cozy bedrooms
with perfect reading lamps. . . .

Barbara Raskin

After love, book collecting is the most exhilarating sport of all.

Abraham Rosenbach

I feel about a hot bath the way
religious people feel about holy water. . . .
The longer I lay there in the hot clear water
the purer I felt, and when I stepped out
at last and wrapped myself in one
of the big, soft, white, hotel bath towels
I felt pure and sweet as a new baby.

Sylvia Plath

I find it wholesome to be alone the greater part of the time. To be in company, even with the best, is soon wearisome and dissipating. I love to be alone. I never found the companion that was so companionable as solitude.

Henry David Thoreau

Learn to be silent. Let your quiet mind listen and absorb.

Pythagoras

The greatest revelation is stillness.

Lao-Tzu

You do not need to leave your room. . . .
Remain sitting at your table and listen.
Do not even listen, simply wait.
Do not even wait, be quite still and solitary.
The world will freely offer itself to you
to be unmasked. It has no choice.
It will roll in ecstasy at your feet.

Franz Kafka

No day is so bad it can't be fixed with a nap.

Carrie Snow

And then there's the smell of perfumed candles, and hot wassail or creamy cocoa on a cold day.

Richard Paul Evans

There is something about holding onto things that I find therapeutic.

Edna O'Brien

Lying in bed would be an altogether perfect and supreme experience
if only one had a coloured pencil long enough to draw on the ceiling.

G. K. Chesterton

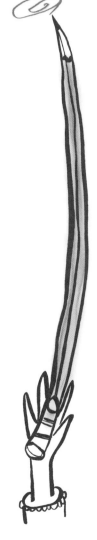

. . . The moment when first you wake up in the morning
is the most wonderful of the twenty-four hours.
No matter how weary or dreary you may feel, you
possess the certainty that . . . absolutely anything
may happen.

Monica Baldwin

I live a day at a time. Each day I look for a kernel of excitement. In the morning,
I say: "What is my exciting thing for today?" Then I do the day.

Barbara Jordan

Life is painting a picture, not doing a sum.

Oliver Wendell Holmes, Jr.

The days that make us happy make us wise.

John Masefield

The morning cup of coffee has an exhilaration
about it which the cheering influence
of the afternoon or evening cup of tea cannot
be expected to produce.

Oliver Wendell Holmes, Sr.

ƒor me, the morning beauty routine is more than just primping, it's a daily opportunity to reflect, fantasize, brainstorm. . . . It's while putting on makeup and doing my hair that I usually get my best ideas, remember something I've forgotten to do, think of something I haven't thought of in years.

Elizabeth Kuster

Never work before breakfast;
if you have to work before breakfast, get your breakfast first.

Josh Billings

*g*et in the habit of removing your shoes before
you enter your house. . . . When you leave your shoes at the door,
you start to feel you can leave your troubles there, too.

Elaine St. James

"Our tea" was as lavish as before,
with lovely thin sandwiches, delicate cookies,
and finely sliced lemon. Care had been
taken. . . . She would not have returned to that era
at any price, but a moment now and then,
feeling like Alice in Wonderland but
at a proper tea party, could be cherished.

Amanda Cross

*L*iving artfully might require taking the time to buy things with soul for the home. Good linens, a special rug, or a simple teapot can be a source of enrichment not only in our own life, but also in the lives of our children and grandchildren.

Thomas Moore

We look too much to museums.
The sun coming up in the morning is enough.

Romare Bearden

Sit in reverie and watch the changing color of the waves that break upon the idle seashore of the mind.

Henry Wadsworth Longfellow

Fishing is much more than fish. . . . It is the great occasion
when we may return to the fine simplicity of our forefathers.

Herbert Hoover

*S*wimming in the river, lazing in the garden, playing tennis, having tea in the shade of some tree because it was too hot anywhere else. . . .

Rosamunde Pilcher

*B*elieve me, my young friend, there is nothing—absolutely nothing—half so much worth doing as simply messing around in boats.

Kenneth Grahame

. . . drifting downstream in a row boat
doesn't count against your life span.

James Patterson

Sailing, like bicycle racing or music, demanded one live a moment at a time.

Ridley Pearson

 I remember riding home on a summer's eve
in the back of an ancient Ford pickup truck,
with two eight-year-old cousins. . . . We'd been
swimming and were sitting on the inner tubes
for comfort, and had a couple of old quilts and
an elderly dog wrapped close for warmth.
We were eating chocolate cookies and drinking
sweet milk out of a Mason jar. . . . Now that's
transportation. The way I like to travel.
Robert Fulghum

I could hear crickets singing and frogs croaking and all the other gentle night sounds of the country. I felt as though I were in another more immense, never-ending world, and wished I could keep riding forever to the ends of the earth.

Yoshiko Uchida

What we loved best about England was the grass—
the short, clean, incredibly green grass with its underlying tough,
springy turf, three hundred years growing.

Han Suyin

The sum of the whole is this:
walk and be happy; walk and be healthy.

Charles Dickens

The true charm of pedestrianism does not lie in the walking, or in the scenery, but in the talking.

Mark Twain

*G*o to a local grove to pick fruit and then go home
and cook something wonderful with it.

Cyndi Haynes and Dale Edwards

My oasis? My front porch. It's dark, screened
and partially obscured by forsythia bushes—
the perfect place to see without being seen.
I can people-watch, listen to the sound
of the leaves and the creak of the porch swing,
or simply enjoy the cool breeze.

Salli Rasberry and Padi Selwyn

When I garden, I set out to do one thing and pretty soon I'm doing something else. This meandering—a kind of free association between earth, tools, body and mind— is, for me, an act of meditation.

Ann Raver

If I were a maker of perfumes, I would make one and call it "Spring,"
and it would smell like this cool, sweet, early-morning air.

Ann Petry

On clear evenings, lie on a blanket
in your backyard and really look at the night sky.
Gazing at the stars reminds us that
there's more to life than we'll ever realize and
that every day brings new chances.

Sarah Ban Breathnach

I lived once in the American desert. The solitude opens up.
It becomes an enormous surrounding comfort.

Vivian Gornick

Choose such pleasures as recreate and cost little.

Thomas Fuller

When we can share—that is poetry in the prose of life.

Sigmund Freud

The most useless day of all is that in which we have not laughed.

Sebasteine Chamfort